GUIDED BY LOVE

Navigating Life with a Mother with Memory Loss

SARAH CION AND
ELIZABETH HELLER

FOREWORD BY MURRAY CION, MD.

CONTENTS

DEDICATION

This book is dedicated to Fatouma, Flor, and Marie LaRose, my mother's wonderful home attendants who work selflessly, lovingly, and tirelessly each and every day.

Special thanks to Robert, Matthew, Denice and Hokuaoka'ale Gilman, Gwen Manning, Lara and Lorenzo Palombi, Erik Shea, Peter and Kim Cion, Murray Cion, Audrey Welber, Kathleen Hart, Eleaser Singletary, Audrey Swanson, Ellen Joan Henschel, Christine Puente, Carolyn Sheltraw, and Beatriz Lugo-Gonzalez and staff of The Westchester Center for Independent and Assisted Living.

FRIDAY

BEAUTIFUL FUTIMA

FOREWORD

As a psychiatrist who specializes in the care of the elderly, I have seen firsthand the toll that dementia can take on both patients and their caregivers. It is a devastating disease that can leave families feeling lost, overwhelmed, and alone. That's why I was so grateful when Sarah approached me about writing this foreword. As someone who has lived through the experience of caring for a loved one with dementia, Sarah has a unique perspective on the challenges and rewards of this journey.

In this book, Sarah shares her personal story of caring for her mother through the maze of dementia. She shares the emotions, struggles, and triumphs of this journey, as well as the practical tips and strategies that she has found helpful in managing the daily challenges of caring for someone with dementia.

Having read this book I was struck by Sarah's honesty and vulnerability. She doesn't shy away from the difficult moments or the painful emotions that come with caring for someone she loves with dementia. But she also shares the moments of joy and connection that are possible, even in the midst of dealing with this disease.

What I appreciate most about this book is that it is not just a memoir or a collection of tips. It is a heartfelt exploration of what it means to care for someone with dementia. It is a reminder that we are all human, and that we all need love, support, and compassion, especially when we are faced with the challenges of aging and illness. I believe that this book will be a valuable resource for anyone who is caring for a loved one with dementia. It provides practical advice and guidance, but it also offers hope and inspiration. It is a reminder that, even in the darkest moments, there is still light to be found. I am grateful to Sarah for sharing her story with us. I hope that it will bring comfort, support, and guidance to all those who are on this difficult journey.

Maurice Cion, MD.

INTRODUCTION

Dementia is a debilitating illness that affects millions of people worldwide. It is a chronic, progressive condition that affects memory, thinking, behavior, and the ability to carry out daily activities. The disease affects not only the person diagnosed with it but also their loved ones, who are often responsible for providing care and support.

This book is a personal account of the caregiver's experience on a journey with a loved one with dementia and all the challenges, emotions, and experiences that come with caring for a loved one with dementia.

In this book, I will share my story of caring for my mother, who was diagnosed with dementia in her early 80s. I will share the ups and downs, the joys and frustrations, and the laughter and tears of our journey together. I will also share the practical tips, strategies, and resources that I have found helpful in managing the daily challenges of caring for someone with dementia.

Ultimately, caregivers should remember that they are doing an important and selfless job and that their efforts are appreciated, even if their loved one may not be able to express this themselves.

GROWING OLD
by Elizabeth Heller

Just growing old can surely be tough
Some times are smooth and others rough
To think that's so is delusion's dream
And things aren't always what they seem
Love is catchy—spreads—explodes
Will take us through some foreign roads!
Life gives joy when love comes first
Gives hope and courage to end all thirst
Love is the answer to care and woes
Love sends shivers to hearts and toes
Love is constant—love will stay
Love will never go away
Love's here forever—believe it's so
Through wind, rain, frost, and turbulent snow
It's love to rescue all at last
The fruits will come—and end the fast
Love is present—will never give up
And therein lies our loving cup!

CHAPTER 1

TRUE LOVE

My mom and Robert in 1957

When my mom attended Boston University in 1957, she met a young man named Robert. He was very into photography and quite taken with my mom, so much so that he created a photo of them by superimposing his high school photo over hers. She was charmed by the gift and its thoughtfulness, and the two began to date.

However, my grandfather would not hear of this relationship. Robert wanted to be a filmmaker, and my Grampa Max did not think this was a suitable profession for any husband of his daughter. So he enrolled her at the University of Pennsylvania and strongly encouraged her to marry Murray Cion, a young physician in training there. To say she was ambivalent was an understatement—family legend says she crossed out the wedding date five times on the invitations before she finally married my father. Though only 21, my grandparents were quite eager to marry her off—to a doctor.

Fortunately, for me, she married him! My parents had me and my brother in 1964 in 1964 and 1967 respectively, and stayed married until they went their separate ways in 1985, the same year I left for college

After the divorce, my mother found joy in hanging out with her "chick friends" in suburban Massachusetts, substitute teaching at the local high school, and swimming at the local gym. She had a good life as a single lady, enjoying the company of various man friends over the years. However, I always wished that she would find true love again. I think she did too because when I would bring it up she would always say, "Hope springs eternal!"

Many years later, my mother started talking about Robert, and their times in college. She told me that Robert had contacted her and shared that his wife of 50 years had passed and wondered how my mom was. Soon, he was asking her to consider visiting him in Maui. My mother came back from that trip more alive than I'd ever seen her before, and I was so excited for her! Soon after, Robert asked my mother if she would consider selling her house and moving to Maui to be with him.

She was overwhelmed by the decision to leave my brother and me. She asked me if she should, and without hesitation, I said, "Do it, this is your swan song! Grab it by the horns and go! Go find true love!"

We spent the next few weeks cleaning her home and selling her antiques. We put a lot in storage and sent a few small suitcases to Hawaii because it was so warm there. She really didn't need much.

My mother was blissfully happy with Robert, it was a wonderful life. My brother and I made a point to go visit every year. Things were going smoothly!

By their third year together, Robert had some decline in his vision and decided to stop driving. We also started to see signs of my mom losing her memory a bit but we didn't think much of it. For instance, I would notice several missed calls on my phone accompanied by duplicate messages within a short period of time.

One day we received a call from the bank. My mother had withdrawn $14,500 in cash and had ostensibly given it to this man she was meeting over the course of three days. A phone scammer called her flip phone, threatening to harm my brother if she did not meet them at the bank and give them cash. She didn't remember that she had already given him money, and he took full advantage of that. It was then that we knew we really had an issue on our hands.

We quickly secured my mother's remaining funds. We hired a young lady a few hours a week to take my mom and Robert grocery shopping, to do some light cooking, and to take walks with my mother, etc. Though the situation was worrisome, Robert's wonderful family lived nearby and they kept an eye on the two of them as best they could.

One day Robert's son called to let us know Robert wasn't feeling well. Robert was not the type of guy to go to hospitals or doctors but was told his kidneys were failing. He was given the choice of dialysis a few times a week at the doctor's office, or alternatively, having a catheter put in so he could stay home and receive insulin while he slept. He didn't want either. Robert always lived the way he wanted to, and we supported him. He ultimately decided to pass on medical intervention and within the month hospice was there. On May 5, 2022, Robert passed away quietly in his home—next to my mother.

My brother and I quickly had to figure out what to do. We decided that my mom would live with me. My brother would go to Maui and get her while I prepared my home. I installed a grab bar and safe seat for the shower and cleared out my bedroom so she didn't have to go up and down the stairs to get to the kitchen. Being displaced from my living space was disconcerting, as well as the overwhelming feeling of all the unknowns that were to accompany this new life shift.

My mother arrived on my doorstep on May 13, 2022. I hadn't seen her since the previous summer and I had the shock of my life when I realized how impaired her memory had gotten. She had three cavities. Her glasses were fogged over and she couldn't hear me. I quickly started making appointments. We went to the optometrist and got her new glasses. We went to the dentist and she got three new crowns. We went to the audiologist and got her fitted for hearing aids. I was happy to be getting her all fixed up, but it was becoming very clear that I needed help. I could not do this by myself! By this point, my mother had about a three-second memory retention. I likened it to The Marauder's Map from Harry Potter—as soon as the viewer would look at the map it would dissipate and become a blank page. This is exactly how my mother's memory operated. Thoughts only remained for a few moments.

In a strange way, I was surprised and delighted that she no longer remembered the negatives that had plagued her over the years due to a painful divorce. That was one positive aspect of this—she only remembered good things and for that, I was grateful! Prior to that, really for much of my adult life, I only heard my mom's sad and upsetting stories which were hurtful to me because my father and I always had a very close relationship. What a humorous dichotomy to now only hear "Your father is such a nice man!" and, "What a good father he's been, I wouldn't mind having dinner with him sometime!"

Each day was like Groundhog Day. My mom would wake up and ask the same questions, usually starting with asking what had happened to Robert. At first, I told the truth—that he had passed on but it upset her so much and then I'd feel sad for hours each day. This is when I realized I had absolutely no training on how to deal with this issue. So I did what every person born in 1967 would do—I Googled it!

What should you not say to a parent with dementia?

Google said:

1) Don't tell them they are wrong about something
2) Don't argue with them
3) Don't ask if they remember something
4) Don't remind them that their spouse, parent, or other loved one is dead
5) Don't bring up topics that may upset them

To my dismay, I learned I was doing many things wrong! I knew I needed professional help.

I found a support group and started my journey with the three home attendants to help me care for my mother. They could not have come at a better time because I was at my wit's end. Fatouma would come Wednesday through Saturday, Flor would come on Sundays, and Marie LaRose would come on Mondays and Tuesdays. It took a few weeks to solidify the schedule, but eventually, we all settled into a nice rhythm. I asked my mom to write down what it was like to have a home attendant every day. Here is what she wrote:

• • • • • • •

What it's Like to Have a "Home Attendant" Come Every Day

by Elizabeth Heller

Wow! A HOME attendant! Someone who can come in and in a split second review what needs to be polished, combed, moved, removed, reset, recolored, puffed up, and completely renewed!

She pushes you aside to remake your already made bedclothes and bedroom comforter while she straightens and neatens and rearranges every article and lamp and chair and window shade and table and pillows and rugs and wall hangings and family pictures that color and shine and spiffy up the entire room. Room by room she flies through the various articles like a volcano in process. And piece by piece and bit by bit does her bidding and rearranging with zest and utter focusing — a tornado indeed! Whoa!

Puzzles, walks, food, furniture, and anything that beautifies the room to your liking are immediately recolored and resigned to some other space or being. Is this the home that has comforted and sheltered you for so many years? "Umpossible" or "ooompossible" as my father-in-law used to boast! Yes, it is so—impossible—and so the space is virtually and unforgettably and remarkably and completely renewed—to be continued!!!!

P.S. We grow to love the space which now is organized and neat and very very well situated with each and every chair, table, and window hanging in its proper space and place! A miracle in the making: a miracle INDEED!

. . . .

I realized that my mother had a talent for writing, so I got her some blank notebooks for writing down thoughts and poems. I also got sketch pads because that was something that she still loved to do. She made drawings of Fatouma, Flor, and Marie LaRose every day, which delighted them. She also really enjoyed word puzzles and crocheting, so I kept these activities on the kitchen table to keep my mother busy. She also got outside for daily walks with the home attendants.

After all the effort to get my mother set up with good care, I felt like I'd become fluent in "Alzheimer's

Caregiver." I understand so much more now than when my mother arrived here. Today it's clear to me that my mother must stay in the present moment, nothing more, nothing less. But what she has become, is pure love. If I get frustrated, angry, or upset, I always get another chance. Life has been distilled down to one truth—and that is love.

I hope this book provides comfort to those going through this journey. Getting help is the most important thing, I believe, for a caregiver—so please take care of yourself first and foremost. I have provided a list of resources at the back of the book to help guide the way. Navigating life with a mother with memory loss is a journey that is both heartwarming and heartbreaking—all at once. But love is our guide.

My mom and Robert in 2017 reunited after 60 years

A REAL BLESSING

by Elizabeth Heller

I am blessed to be here with Lara, Lorenzo, Sarah, and any friends that care to spend time with me. We can walk, talk, or do whatever we wish. Now that is a real blessing! I feel surrounded by caring loved ones and friends, and what more can one ask for? To be and surround myself with others with whatever we wish to do. I am here to enjoy the friends family and good cheer and weather, love, and camaraderie. Such love is a privilege and a joy! To love and be loved, what more can anyone ask? To live, love, and be! To walk, talk, do puzzles if I wish, dream, and just live! Yay! Sometimes we just like to be quiet and enjoy the day, the wind, and the environment. And sometimes it is a joy just to be quiet and reflective. Voila! We needn't have to do something at all times. We love quiet reflective times as well.

CHAPTER 2

THE DIAGNOSIS

I still remember the day my mother was diagnosed with dementia. It was a bright and sunny day in early summer, and we were in her doctor's office. My mother had been experiencing memory problems for some time The doctor explained that my mother had a form of memory loss called Alzheimer's disease. He explained the symptoms, the progression, and the available treatments. I listened carefully, trying to absorb everything he was saying. When the doctor finished, my mother turned to me with tears in her eyes. "What does this mean?" she asked me. "It means that you have a disease that affects your memory and thinking," I said gently. "But we'll figure it out together. We'll get you the help you need." And so began our journey.

When my mother first began showing signs of memory loss, I didn't think much of it. I figured it was just a normal part of aging. But as time went on, her forgetfulness became more pronounced. She would repeat the same stories over and over again and struggle to remember the names of close family members. It was difficult to watch her struggle, and I knew that something was not right. Her doctor recommended she undergo a series of tests to determine the cause of her memory loss. This was an ordeal for my mother. She struggled with cognitive comprehension and became frustrated when she couldn't remember the answers. But we persevered, and after several weeks we finally received a diagnosis: dementia. The diagnosis was not a shock to us. I had heard of dementia before, as it had happened to my grandmother years earlier.

As we began to come to terms with the diagnosis, I realized that there were several things that I needed to do in order to help my mother and our family navigate this new reality. The first thing was to educate myself about the disease. I read books, articles, and online resources about dementia and Alzheimer's disease. I learned that dementia is a progressive disease that affects the brain, leading to a decline in cognitive function, memory loss, and other symptoms. I found that there are several different types of dementia, each with its own set of symptoms and challenges.

I attended support groups and workshops to learn more about how to care for someone with dementia. I also made sure that my mother received the medical care and support that she needed. We found a specialist who could provide us with guidance and advice on how to manage her symptoms and maintain her quality of life.

But perhaps the most important thing that I did was to talk openly and honestly with my children about the diagnosis. They needed to understand what was happening to their grandmother and to our family. We had open conversations so we could ask questions, express fears and concerns, and support each other through this difficult time. As we began to adjust to the new reality of my mother's diagnosis, I also began to see the importance of living in the present moment. Dementia is a progressive disease, and there is no cure. But that doesn't mean that life is over.

We focused on the things that we could still enjoy together. We went for walks, listened to music, and spent time with friends and family. We made new memories and cherished the ones that we had. The diagnosis of dementia was a difficult moment for our family, but it was also a turning point. It forced us to confront the reality of my mother's illness and to make changes in our lives. But it also reminded us of the importance of love, support, and compassion, especially in times of difficulty.

As we continue on this journey with my mother, I am grateful for the lessons that we have learned and the love that we share. The diagnosis of dementia was not the end of our story, but rather the beginning of a new chapter.

NO ONE IS PERFECT

by Elizabeth Heller

Criticism is always welcome
And taken to the core
We all are living life together
To share our love forevermore
It certainly isn't "Me" "My" or "I"
But quite the opposite
Thank God for the sun, the stars, and the rain
For nature will never quit
We, humble humans, live on earth
To breathe God-given air
To help each other tenderly
With delight and heartful care
We're here on earth to live with zest
With grateful harmony
To give our thanks to God each day
And wisdom to be FREE!

FRIDAY FEB 17 2023

Kind & Beautiful
FATUMA

CHAPTER 3

THE NEW NORMAL

As we began to adjust to a new normal, I needed to now learn about the stages of the disease, the behaviors that are common in people with dementia, and the strategies for managing them.

I made changes to my mother's living arrangements, moving her into my bedroom on the first floor so that I could provide the care she needed. I made modifications to my home to make it safe and accessible for her, such as installing grab bars in the bathroom and removing tripping hazards. As we settled into our new routine, I learned that caring for someone with dementia requires a great deal of patience and flexibility. I had to learn to adapt to my mother's changing needs and abilities and to be patient with her when she became confused or frustrated.

It was not easy, but over time, we learned to adapt and find new ways of living that allowed us to support my mother and each other. One of the first things we had to adjust to was my mother's changing needs. As her dementia progressed, she needed more and more assistance with everyday tasks. Things that we had taken for granted, like cooking a meal or getting dressed, became difficult for her.

At first, we tried to do everything ourselves, but we quickly realized that it wasn't sustainable. We needed to find a way to balance my mother's needs with our own. We worked with my mother's doctors and caregivers to develop a plan that would meet her requirements and allow us to continue living our own lives. We hired home attendants to help my mother with some of her daily tasks, like cooking and cleaning. We also installed safety features like handrails in the bathroom and a medical alert system.

We also had to come to terms with the emotional impact of my mother's illness. Watching her struggle, we often felt helpless and overwhelmed. We had to learn to accept that there were some things that we could not change and focus on the things that we could.

One of the most important things we did to adjust to the new normal was to ask for support from others. We joined support groups and connected with other families who were going through similar experiences. We also reached out to friends and extended family members who offered their love and support during this difficult time. We began to focus on the things that we could still enjoy together. We went on outings and took part in activities that my mother enjoyed. We also celebrated holidays and special occasions, even if they were not the same as they used to be.

Through it all, we learned that adjusting to the new normal was a process. It took time, patience, and understanding. But we also learned that it was possible to find joy and meaning in this new way of living. We learned to appreciate the small moments of happiness and cherish the time that we had left with my mother.

As we continue on this journey, we know that there will be more challenges to come. But we also know that we are not alone. We have each other and a community of people who care about us. And we have the strength and resilience to face whatever comes our way.

Meals had become a particular challenge between my mother and me. Not only did she only want to eat what I was eating, she needed to eat it at the same time as me. As a professional musician, I eat at very odd times, so our schedules and meal times did not always coincide.

Here are some strategies that helped us through this particular situation:

1. Be prepared: Anticipate their needs and preferences by planning ahead for mealtime. If your loved one likes the same foods as you, try to prepare enough for both of you. If possible, prepare their meal first so they can eat without having to wait for you.

2. Establish a routine: Routines can be helpful for someone with memory loss. Try to set regular meal times and stick to them as much as possible. This helps your loved one anticipate meal times and reduces anxiety around mealtime.

3. Offer alternatives: If they only want to eat what you are eating, consider offering

her some alternatives that are similar. For example, if you are having tofu and veggies, offer a similar meal, such as chicken and potatoes. This may help your loved one to feel included in the meal while still giving them some choice.

4. Be patient and compassionate: Remember that upsetting behavior is a result of memory loss, and not deliberate. Try to be patient and compassionate, even when it's difficult. Offer reassurance and comfort, and try to find ways to make mealtimes pleasant for both of you.

FOR RUTH AND STEPHEN WITH LOVE AND THANKS

by Elizabeth Heller

What a glorious, joyful, and remarkable eve
The last day of September I do believe
The host and hostess were extraordinarily
gracious
The home was elegant, but not ostentatious
We felt the love, such a delicious dinner!
One could not imagine a more gourmet
winner!
Peter, Sarah, and Kim were there
To enjoy the energy and lovely fare
Thank you, dear Ruth and Stephen—much
love
We are grateful and thankful for someone
above
I do think there's a God to see us through
I'm not religious but believe it's true!
There is someone above who thinks of us
He's there but does not make a fuss.
Quietly there for love and care
So I thank him for family and for being there!

CHAPTER 4

COMMUNICATION

As dementia progresses, communication becomes increasingly challenging, and both the caregiver and the person with dementia can become frustrated, leading to misunderstandings and conflict.

One of the most problematic aspects of caring for my mother with dementia was communication. Her illness made it difficult for her to express herself and understand what was happening around her. She would often struggle to find the right words or to express herself clearly. We had to learn new ways of communicating with her. I learned to connect with my mother on an emotional level, rather than relying on verbal communication. This required vulnerability and openness on both sides, as we had to learn to understand each other's emotions and needs without words. We relied on visual cues and gestures more and more to convey our meaning and practiced patience and understanding when my mother became confused or agitated. It was not her fault that she was struggling with her memory, and we had to remind ourselves of this when we became frustrated.

When my mother couldn't get her point across, she'd experience agitation or even aggression. This can happen when the person with memory loss becomes overwhelmed or confused. I learned to recognize the signs of agitation so I could intervene early to prevent it from escalating.

Dementia affects communication in a number of ways. As the disease progresses, it can impair a person's ability to understand and use language. They may struggle to find the right words, have difficulty following a conversation, or repeat themselves frequently. They may also lose the ability to communicate through body language or facial expressions, making it even harder for caregivers to understand their needs and emotions. They may have trouble finding the right words to express themselves or understanding what others are saying. They may also repeat themselves, become agitated or confused, or lose track of the conversation. This can make it difficult for the caregiver to understand what the person with dementia needs or wants.

One of the key strategies for improving communication with someone with dementia is to use simple, clear language. Avoid using complicated sentences or idioms, as these can be confusing. Speak slowly and clearly, and try to use concrete examples when explaining things. For example, instead of saying "We're going to the store," say "We're going to buy groceries". This can help your loved one better understand what you're saying.

Also, pay attention to your own nonverbal communication. People with dementia are often very sensitive to nonverbal cues, and if you're feeling anxious or upset, they may pick up on that and become agitated themselves. Try to project a sense of calm and reassurance, even if you're feeling stressed.

Another important aspect of communication in dementia caregiving is understanding the person's individual needs and preferences. Dementia affects everyone differently, and it's important to tailor your communication approach to the person's specific needs. For example, some people with dementia may respond better to visual cues, while others may prefer written instructions. By understanding your loved one's unique communication style, you can better meet their needs and reduce frustration. In some cases, technology such as picture boards or voice-activated assistants can be helpful in improving communication with someone with dementia. These devices can be particularly helpful for people who struggle with language.

It's also important to remember that communication is a two-way street. Your loved one with dementia may have difficulty expressing their thoughts and feelings. Encourage them to communicate in whatever way they can, whether that's through words, gestures, or facial expressions. Listen carefully to what they have to say and try to respond in a way that shows that you understand.

When communication becomes particularly difficult, it can be helpful to take a break and come back to the conversation later. This can give both you and your loved one a chance to regroup and approach the conversation with a fresh perspective. It's also important to remember that there will be good days and bad days. Some days your loved one may be more responsive than others, and it's important to be patient and flexible.

It's also important to be aware of potential triggers that can exacerbate communication difficulties. For example, loud noises or chaotic environments can be overwhelming for someone with dementia and make communication more challenging. By creating a calm and comfortable environment, you can help your loved one better focus on communication and reduce stress.

It is vital to remember that communication is not just about conveying information—it's also about maintaining social connections and emotional bonds. Even when verbal communication becomes difficult, it's important to continue to engage with your loved one in ways that promote connection and emotional closeness. It's also important to continue to engage in activities that you and your loved one enjoy, such as listening to music or going for walks together.

Although communication can be one of the biggest challenges of dementia caregiving, remember that there are strategies and techniques that can help. Seeking out support, understanding your loved one's individual needs, and creating a calm and comfortable environment can all help improve communication. By focusing on these simple strategies you can help your loved one feel supported and cared for throughout their journey with dementia.

In conclusion, caring for someone with dementia can be emotionally and physically exhausting, and it's easy to neglect your own needs in the process. Make sure you're getting enough rest, eating well, and engaging in activities that bring you joy. This can help you better cope with the challenges of communication and caregiving in general.

GIVING THANKS

by Elizabeth Heller

Dementia, dementia—we all grow old
Some retreat—and others are bold
But however, it is or who you may be
Nobody's pure as gold — you'll see!
Some forget—some lose their way
Forget if it is night or day
But we'll make it with "live, love, and pray"
With love in our hearts
And smiles each day
We're lucky to have loving children I say!
And grandkids with smarts and joyous smiles
That way we'll be moving for miles
Helpers with magical treasures we have
They really truly do their part
Make happy the lonely—give care where it's
needed
And turn working into an art
We bless each day, each dog and cat
Who can ever, ever beat that?
For animals are creatures with foresight and
dreams

They provide us with joy from sunlight to moonbeams
The love each day of which we're aware
We'll make it all right with family who care
Thankful for our minds to remember
From winter to spring, from May to December
May everyone everywhere be thankful
For our minds alert and our tanks are full!

CHAPTER 5

REPETITION

Caring for a loved one with memory loss can be a difficult and challenging journey. One of the common challenges caregivers face is dealing with repetitive behaviors or statements that their loved one may exhibit. It can be frustrating, and even annoying, to hear the same thing over and over again, but it is important to approach these situations with empathy and understanding. This repetition often referred to as "perseveration," is a common symptom of dementia and can be emotionally exhausting for the caregiver.

At first, the repetition may not seem like a big deal, but as the hours and days go on, it can begin to wear on the caregiver's patience and emotional well-being. Caregivers feel trapped in a never-ending cycle of answering the same questions, responding to the same comments, and hearing the same stories over and over again.

It's important for caregivers to remember that their loved one is not intentionally trying to be difficult or annoying. This behavior is a result of the changes happening in their brain due which can affect an individual's ability to remember things or to control their behavior. Repetitive behaviors and statements are common in memory loss and are often a way for your loved one to communicate their needs or emotions.

There are some strategies that can help manage the frustration of repetition when caring for someone with memory loss. One approach is to try and redirect the conversation to a different topic or activity. This can help break the cycle of repetition and engage the person in a different way. For example, if they keep asking about a particular event, you could try talking about a different event or activity that they enjoy.

Another strategy is to use visual aids or reminders to help reduce the need for repetition. For example, you could place notes around the house reminding your loved one of important information or write down a daily schedule of activities to help them remember what they need to do. It can also be helpful to establish a routine and stick to it as much as possible. This can help reduce anxiety and confusion, which can lead to repetitive behavior.

Validation is another technique that caregivers can use. This involves acknowledging the person's feelings and concerns, even if you've heard them before. For example, if they keep asking about a particular family member who has passed away, instead of trying to correct them, you could say something like, "I know how much you miss them. They were such an important part of your life."

Another helpful approach is to engage in activities that your loved one enjoys, such as listening to music, looking at photo albums, or going for a walk. These activities can help distract from repetitive behaviors and provide a sense of enjoyment and purpose.

When dealing with repetitive behaviors or statements, it can be easy to become impatient or condescending toward your loved one. Try to remember that your loved one is not intentionally being annoying or difficult. They are simply struggling with memory loss, and it is important to approach these situations with empathy and understanding. If you do become frustrated, it is important to take responsibility for your actions and apologize if necessary. Remember, it is okay to make mistakes, but it is important to learn from them and to approach similar situations in a more positive and constructive way in the future.

Another way to avoid being condescending is to take a break when you feel your frustration building up. It is okay to step away from the situation for a few minutes to collect yourself and come back with a fresh perspective.

In summary, dealing with the repetition that often comes with caring for someone with memory loss can be emotionally challenging for caregivers. However, by approaching the situation with empathy, validation, and engagement in enjoyable activities, and by taking care of their own well-being, caregivers can help reduce frustration and provide the best possible care for their loved one.

THE ORCHID
by Elizabeth Heller

The orchid is a very delicate living creature. It only wants to be watered when its soul says "yes" to watering. It is alive and has a mind of its own. We must respect the wishes and desires of all our precious living beings. One ice cube every three weeks to keep it well and alive. It is a beautiful and intelligent being and deserves our complete and thorough attention. All living creatures deserve complete and total respect—they are human too!

CHAPTER 6

DENIAL

Denial is a common defense mechanism that people use to cope with difficult situations. When someone is diagnosed with dementia, it can be overwhelming to them, and going into denial can be a way to avoid facing the reality of the situation. This often leads the individual with dementia to refuse to acknowledge their disease, preferring instead to downplay or ignore their symptoms. This, of course, makes it much more difficult for caregivers to provide adequate care, not to mention the frustration it can cause. The most important lesson here is to be empathetic and to listen to the person with memory loss, this may help them accept what is happening in that moment.

Another way denial shows up is in refusal of help or support. The person with dementia may not want to seem weak or vulnerable, so maintaining respect for the person with dementia is crucial. This was a big source of conflict between my mother and me. I would explain to her that she needed assistance, but my mother would refuse, saying she could do everything on her own. This led to a constant battle between myself and my mother, with me feeling like my mother was being stubborn and my mother feeling like I was trying to take away her independence.

One difficult aspect of denial in dementia is the way it can manifest as a cover-up for embarrassment. For example, an individual with dementia may forget the things you've told them and then deny having forgotten them. This denial can be especially frustrating for caregivers as the individual with dementia may become defensive or even angry when confronted about their forgetfulness, leading to a breakdown in communication and potentially damaging the caregiver-patient relationship.

My own experience with my mother's denial is a perfect example of how frustrating it can be. My mother would often forget little things like me asking her to please not water my orchid, and then deny that she had watered it, or she would insist that she didn't need any help, despite the fact that she was clearly struggling with daily tasks. This led to me feeling like my mother wasn't respecting my wishes and directives. However, I soon realized that my mother's denial was a defense mechanism to protect herself from the fear and anxiety of forgetting important things.

Denial can also manifest in more subtle ways, such as a reluctance to discuss the future or make plans for long-term care. Individuals with dementia may avoid discussions about their condition or dismiss concerns about their ability to live independently. This denial can be driven by a fear of losing control or a desire to avoid thinking about the future. However, avoiding these important conversations only makes it more difficult for caregivers to plan for their loved one's long-term care once the decisions become more imminent.

In addition to these specific examples, denial can have a broader impact on individuals with dementia and their caregivers. Denial can lead to a breakdown

in communication and trust, making it more difficult for caregivers to provide necessary care and
support. It can also lead to feelings of frustration
and helplessness, as caregivers struggle to manage
their loved one's condition while also navigating the
challenges of denial. This can be particularly challenging for family members who may be struggling
with their own emotions and grief over their loved
one's condition.

Another important step is to address denial directly,
using open and honest communication. Caregivers
can try to help their loved ones understand the
consequences of denial and the importance of
accepting help and support. One such strategy is
to use simple and clear language. This can help the
person with dementia understand what is being
said and reduce confusion. Additionally, caregivers
can use non-verbal cues, such as facial expressions
or gestures, to help convey meaning.

Caregivers can also try to address the underlying
causes of denial, such as fear, embarrassment, or a
desire for independence. For example, if an individual with dementia is refusing to use a walker or
wheelchair, caregivers can try to find ways to make

these devices more appealing and less stigmatizing. They can also help to build the individual's confidence by providing positive reinforcement and support.

In conclusion, denial is a common response to a diagnosis of dementia, and it can manifest in a variety of ways, including as a cover-up for embarrassment. Denial can have serious consequences for individuals with dementia and their caregivers, making it more difficult to provide necessary care and support. However, by acknowledging and addressing denial directly, caregivers can help their loved ones to accept their condition and receive the care they need. By prioritizing self-care and support, caregivers can also help to manage their own emotions and cope with the challenges of caring for someone with dementia.

Caring for someone with dementia can be emotionally and physically draining, and caregivers need to prioritize their own well-being. This may include seeking help from family and friends, joining a support group, or seeking professional help.

I DIDN'T DO IT!
by Elizabeth Heller

I write and I walk I talk and I listen
And respond with ease and to please
But sometimes I do not remember
some things and say, "It was not me!"
My brain plays tricks sometimes and things
Are not what they may always seem
I may staunchly say "Not me!"
For my brain does playful things
Like a child playing hide and seek
The fleeting memory always schemes
And I am doubtful that it may surely
Have been I who had such silly dreams
But alas alack it in fact it WAS
Yes, it was actually I, oh my...
Sincerely I'm on track but true
I DID do it but I can't recall...
Is it fall?
September, October, November? December?
Sometimes I cannot seem to remember!

CHAPTER 7

THE EMOTIONAL TOLL

Caring for a loved one with dementia can be emotionally taxing for caregivers. As the disease progresses, caregivers may experience a range of emotions such as guilt, grief, anger, frustration, and helplessness. In this chapter, we will explore the emotional toll of caregiving and strategies to manage caregiver stress and improve emotional well-being.

Caregivers often experience guilt - for not doing enough, not doing things correctly, or needing a break. Caregivers may also feel guilt about the emotions they experience, such as frustration or anger, towards their loved one. These feelings are a normal part of caregiving, and it's important to remember that as caregivers, we are doing the best we can under difficult circumstances.

Grief is another common emotion experienced by caregivers of people with dementia. As the disease progresses, caregivers may experience a sense of loss as their loved one's personality and abilities change. This grief can be compounded by the fact that the person with dementia may still be physically present but no longer the same person they once were. It's important for caregivers to recognize the grief they are experiencing and seek support to help them process these emotions.

Anger and frustration are also common emotions experienced by caregivers. They may feel angry about the unfairness of the situation or frustrated by the challenges of caregiving. It's important to find healthy ways to express these emotions, such as talking to a friend or therapist, practicing relaxation techniques, or engaging in physical activity.

Helplessness is another emotion commonly experienced by caregivers. Caregivers may feel helpless as they watch their loved one's abilities decline. It's important to remember that while there may not be a cure for dementia, there are still things caregivers can do to support their loved one and improve their quality of life. This may include engaging in activities the person enjoys, creating a safe and comfortable environment, and seeking out resources and support.

In addition to these emotions, caregiving can also take a toll on physical health. Caregivers may experience fatigue, insomnia, and other physical symptoms due to the demands of caregiving. It's important for caregivers to take care of themselves by getting enough rest, eating well, and engaging in physical activity. Caregivers should also prioritize their own healthcare needs by keeping up with their own healthcare.

Caring for someone with dementia can be emotionally draining. It can be difficult to watch a loved one's decline and to witness their struggles. I often found myself feeling overwhelmed, frustrated, and sad. It was important for me to take care of myself during this time. I made sure to take breaks when I needed them, to reach out for support from family and friends, and to prioritize my own self-care. I also learned to accept help when it was offered. I had a tendency to want to do everything myself, but I soon realized that I couldn't do it alone. I was grateful for the help and support of my family and friends, who were always there to lend a hand.

One of the issues I faced was my mother's repeated asking if she could help me. While my mother's willingness to assist was admirable, it was also quite frustrating, especially as I was already overwhelmed with my own daily life as well as caregiving responsibilities.

It is common to feel annoyed or even resentful with continual offers for help because it can create an additional burden for you. You may have to take time to explain what needs to be done, supervise work, or even what was done incorrectly. This can cause more frustration as it often creates more work for the caregiver.

It's important to remember that the person with dementia's desire to help is likely coming from a place of love and a desire to contribute to the household. However, you can still communicate your boundaries and limitations while acknowledging her efforts. You might try saying something like, "Thank you so much for wanting to help, Mom. I really appreciate it. Right now, I need to handle this task on my own, but I'll let you know if I need your assistance later."

You may want to consider finding ways for your patient to contribute to the household, by finding tasks within her capabilities, less demanding, and that she can complete without supervision. This the person with memory loss feel valued and useful.

Here are some examples of tasks that your loved one may be able to help with, depending on their abilities:

1. Folding laundry—this is a simple task that can be done while sitting down and can be a great way to feel productive.

2. Sorting mail—your loved one can help sort the mail by separating bills, personal letters, and junk mail. This can help you save time and ensure that important mail is not overlooked.

3. Watering plants—if you have indoor or outdoor plants, your loved one may be able to help water them on a regular basis.

4. Setting the table—helping to set the table for meals can be a great way to involve your loved one in meal preparation.

5. Dusting—dusting furniture is a simple and low-stress task, so it's a good one for your loved one to help with.

6. Preparing simple meals—if your loved one enjoys cooking, they may be able to help with preparing simple meals like sandwiches, salads, or soups.

7. Organizing closets or drawers—having your loved one help you organize your closets or drawers, can be a great way to declutter and create more space.

Remember to keep in mind your loved one's capabilities and limitations when assigning tasks. It's important to ensure that the tasks are not too complex or overwhelming and that they are within their physical and cognitive abilities.

Finally, it's important for caregivers to seek out support from others. I know I keep harping on this, but things like joining a support group, talking to a therapist, or reaching out to friends and family members are imperative for self-care. Support from others can help caregivers feel less isolated, more understood, and better equipped to handle the challenges of caregiving.

In summary, caring for a loved one with dementia can be extremely emotionally challenging, but there are strategies and resources available to help caregivers manage stress and improve emotional well-being. By recognizing and addressing common emotions such as guilt, grief, anger, and helplessness, caregivers can better cope with the challenges of caregiving and maintain their own health and well-being. Please find a 24/7 support hotline number in the resources section at the end of this book.

FOR ERIK AND SARAH TOO WITH LOVE

by Elizabeth Heller

Thank you dear Erik for talking
For understanding and kindness and truth
For grasping the love and speaking with heart
One needn't be a sleuth
To see why my thoughtful daughter
Sees your sparkle and twinkle and care
You're one special guy
and now I see why
that twinkle in eyes is there!
YES—smart as our Ragamuffin kittens
And soft as their delicate fur
It's no wonder why the love in their eye
is the magic that must occur!
It's winter but snow is a comfort
To see the love in the air
Where on earth could one be?
YES—grateful the BRONX—it's there!
Thank God for love, the sun, and the moon
It's early in the morn

It's time to get up before it's too late
It's ALMOST AFTERNOON!

SATURDAY
January 13, 2023 53

Edward Mo FATUMA

CHAPTER 8

ANGER AND RESENTMENT

Dealing with a mother who has memory loss can be a challenging experience, and it is not uncommon to feel anger and resentment toward the situation. It is important to acknowledge these emotions and find healthy ways to cope with them. In this chapter, we will explore the different causes of anger and resentment and ways to deal with these emotions.

One of the primary causes of anger and resentment when dealing with a loved one with memory loss is the feeling of loss. Seeing a loved one slowly lose their memory can feel like a bereavement, and this can trigger feelings of anger and resentment towards the situation. You may feel like you have lost the person you once knew and loved, and this can be a painful and frustrating experience.

Another cause of anger and resentment is the feeling of helplessness. You may feel like there is nothing you can do to help your loved one or improve their condition, and that it's a losing battle. This can be overwhelming and emotionally draining and can become a source of frustration and anger.

Being a caregiver for someone with memory loss can be emotionally exhausting. It can feel like you are constantly on edge, trying to anticipate their needs and respond to their changing behavior. This can lead to feelings of anger and resentment, as caregivers often feel that they are sacrificing their own needs and emotions.

As the person with memory loss becomes increasingly dependent on their loved ones, this can create feelings of resentment. It is important to acknowledge these feelings and find healthy ways to deal with them. Here are some strategies that can help you deal with anger and resentment when dealing with a mother with memory loss:

1. Practice Self-Care: One of the most important things you can do is take care of yourself. This can include getting enough rest, eating

well, and engaging in activities that you enjoy. Taking care of yourself can help you feel more balanced and emotionally grounded, which can help you cope with the challenges of caregiving.

2. Seek Support: It can be helpful to seek support from others who are going through a similar experience. This can include joining a support group or talking to a therapist. Talking to others can help you feel less alone and can provide you with valuable insights and advice.

3. Be Realistic: It is important to be realistic about your loved one's condition and what you can do to help them. Recognize that there may be limitations to what you can do, and this is okay. Focus on what you can do, and try not to let the things you cannot control overwhelm you.

4. Set Boundaries: It is important to set boundaries to protect your own emotional well-being. This can include setting limits on how much time you spend with

your loved one, or how much you take on. Setting boundaries can help you feel more in control of the situation and can prevent feelings of resentment from building up.

5. Practice Forgiveness: It can be helpful to practice forgiveness towards your loved one and yourself. Recognize that memory loss is not something that anyone can control, and try to let go of any feelings of anger or resentment towards the situation. Forgiveness can help you feel more at peace with the situation and can prevent negative emotions from consuming you.

It is also important to recognize that anger and resentment are natural emotions when dealing with a challenging situation like caring for a loved one with memory loss. It is okay to feel these emotions, but it is important to find ways to deal with them in a healthy way so that they do not consume you.

By practicing self-care, seeking support, being realistic, setting boundaries, and practicing forgiveness, you can learn to cope with the challenges of caring for a loved one with memory loss. Remember to be gentle with yourself and to take things one day at a time. With time and practice, you can learn to navigate this difficult situation with grace and compassion

In conclusion, dealing with anger and resentment when caring for a mother with memory loss can be a challenging experience. It is important to acknowledge your emotions and find healthy ways to cope with them. Remember that you are not alone, and there are resources available to help you navigate this difficult situation.

ROY BAILEY
by Elizabeth Heller

A surprise gift of flowers alas he did send
Roy Bailey by name, my new special friend
The blossoms are exotic, a gift of delight
The raindrops of dew were exceedingly bright
But soon the sunshine arrived at the door
Speedy delivery from Bailey—need I say
more?

CHAPTER 9

VULNERABILITY

When caring for a loved one with dementia, vulnerability is an unavoidable feeling. Whether it's watching a once-independent parent struggle to perform basic tasks or witnessing the gradual decline of cognitive abilities, the emotional toll of dementia can leave caregivers feeling exposed and overwhelmed. Yet, it's precisely in these moments of vulnerability that caregivers have the opportunity to connect more deeply with their loved ones and build stronger relationships.

Vulnerability is important in dementia care for several reasons. It can help build a stronger relationship between the caregiver and the person with dementia. By being open and honest about their own feelings, caregivers can create a more authentic and empathetic connection with their loved ones. This vulnerability can help foster a sense of trust and security, and also reduce stress and anxiety, both of which are essential for the well-being of both the caregiver and the person with dementia.

As dementia progresses, communication can become more difficult. As I could no longer rely on verbal cues alone, I learned to connect with my mother on an emotional level. This required vulnerability and openness on both sides, as we had to learn to understand each other's emotions and needs without relying on words.

Here are some examples of how vulnerability can be important for a caregiver:

1. Acknowledge your limitations and seek help when needed. Caregiving can be emotionally and physically exhausting, and it's important to recognize when one needs support and assistance.

2. Share your struggles and emotions with others. Caregiving can be a lonely and isolating experience, and it's important to

connect with others who can offer empathy and support.

3. Be open to learning and growth. Caregiving requires constantly adapting to new situations and challenges, and being willing to learn from mistakes and seek out new information can be crucial.

4. Be willing to ask for forgiveness and make amends. Caregiving can be stressful and can sometimes lead to mistakes or miscommunications. Being vulnerable enough to acknowledge one's mistakes and seek forgiveness can help maintain healthy relationships.

5. Be willing to advocate for oneself and the person being cared for. Caregiving can involve navigating complex healthcare and social systems, and being vulnerable enough to speaking up and assert one's needs and rights can be crucial.

6. Be open to feedback and constructive criticism. Caregiving can involve working

closely with other family members, health-care providers, and social workers, and being vulnerable enough to receive feed-back and criticism can help improve communication and outcomes.

7. Be willing to let go of control and accept help from others. Caregiving can involve taking on a lot of responsibility, and being vulnerable enough to ask for and accept help from others can help lighten the load and promote teamwork.

Be willing to express love and gratitude. Caregiving can be a deeply meaningful and rewarding experi-ence, and being vulnerable enough to express love and gratitude to the person being cared for and to others involved in the care can help foster positive relationships and a sense of purpose.

Vulnerability in dementia care can manifest in dif-ferent ways, such as feeling overwhelmed, helpless, or scared. It's a natural response to the challenges and uncertainties of caring for someone with a progressive and unpredictable disease. However, vulnerability can also be a source of strength and connection. When caregivers allow themselves to be vulnerable and share their feelings with their loved ones, it can help build trust, empathy, and understanding. By acknowledging and accepting their own vulnerability, caregivers can create a safe space for their loved ones to express their own fears and concerns.

By acknowledging and accepting our own vulnerability, caregivers can release some of the pressure to always be strong and in control. This creates a more relaxed and compassionate atmosphere, which can be beneficial for the person with dementia as well. Vulnerability can also help caregivers stay connected to their own emotions and needs. By acknowledging their own vulnerability, caregivers can better understand their own emotions and needs and seek support when necessary.

Caregivers should be aware of the ways dementia can make their loved ones more vulnerable. As cognitive abilities decline, individuals with dementia may become more susceptible to abuse, neglect, and financial exploitation. Caregivers can help protect their loved ones by staying alert to signs of mistreatment and taking steps to prevent harm.

Embracing vulnerability in dementia care can be challenging, but there are strategies that caregivers can use to make it easier:

1. Accept your own vulnerability: The first step in embracing vulnerability is to accept and acknowledge your own feelings of vulnerability. It's okay to feel overwhelmed, scared, or helpless at times. By accepting these feelings, you can create space for them and work through them in a healthy way.

2. When appropriate, share your feelings with your loved one. This can help create a more empathetic and connected relationship. Be honest and open, and encourage your loved one to share their own feelings as well.

3. Practice self-care: Taking care of your own needs is essential for maintaining your emotional well-being. Make time for activities that bring you joy and relaxation, and seek support from friends, family, or a support group when needed.

4. Focus on the present moment: Dementia care can be overwhelming when you focus on the future or the past. Try to stay focused on the present moment and appreciate the small moments of connection and joy that you have with your loved one.

5. Seek professional help: If you're feeling overwhelmed or struggling to cope with the challenges of dementia care, don't hesitate to seek professional help. A therapist or counselor can provide support and guidance for managing difficult emotions and navigating the caregiving journey.

Individuals with dementia may also experience internal vulnerabilities related to their sense of identity, purpose, and self-worth. As memories fade and cognitive abilities decline, individuals with dementia can feel disconnected from their former selves and their social networks. Caregivers can help promote a sense of identity and purpose by engaging their loved ones in activities that align with their interests and values. This can help preserve their sense of self and promote feelings of meaning and fulfillment.

In conclusion, vulnerability is an essential aspect of dementia care. While it can be challenging and uncomfortable, it's also an opportunity for connection, growth, and empathy. By acknowledging and accepting their own vulnerability, caregivers can create a safe and compassionate environment for their loved ones with dementia. It's important for caregivers to prioritize their own emotional well-being and seek support when needed. By embracing vulnerability, caregivers can build stronger relationships with their loved ones and find meaning and purpose in the caregiving journey.

MURRAY'S KNEE

by Elizabeth Heller

The skillful surgeon we all agree
performed a mitzvah on Murray's knee
He's healing and mending and incredibly
soon
He'll be singing the ballads he loves to croon
His knee will bend, and he'll walk with ease
Thank the doctor again and say please!
May we all give thanks!

SUNDAY MARCH 5, 2023

FLOR

CHAPTER 10

JOY IN THE JOURNEY

Despite the challenges of caring for my mother with dementia, there were also moments of joy and connection. I found that it was important to focus on these moments and cherish them. In this chapter, we will explore ways for caregivers to find joy and meaning in the journey of dementia caregiving.

One of the ways that my mother and I connected was through music. My mother had always loved music, and even as her memory declined, she could still remember the lyrics to her favorite songs. I would often play her favorite songs on the piano and we would sing together. It was a beautiful way for us to connect and find joy in the journey.

Another way to find joy in the journey is to focus on the present and appreciate the small moments of joy that can be found in everyday life. This may include enjoying a cup of tea together, listening to music, or taking a walk outside. By focusing on the present moment and enjoying simple pleasures, caregivers can find meaning and purpose in their role as a caregiver.

Yet another way to find joy in the journey is to create opportunities for meaningful engagement and connection. This may include engaging in activities that the person with dementia enjoys, such as listening to music, looking at old photographs, or gentle exercise.

Caregivers can also find social connections by attending support groups (yes, I will keep reminding you) or connecting with other caregivers online. This creates a sense of community and support, which can be invaluable during the journey of caregiving. Caregivers also need to take care of themselves and engage in activities that bring them joy and fulfillment. This may include hobbies, exercise, or spending time with friends and family. By prioritizing their own needs and interests, caregivers can reduce stress and find joy in their own lives, which can, in turn, benefit their loved one. Caregivers can create opportunities for reminiscing life experiences and sharing stories, which can help preserve the person's legacy and create meaningful moments of connection.

Turning focus onto the person with dementia's remaining abilities and strengths, instead of dwelling on what the person can no longer do, helps caregivers to focus on what they can still do and find ways to support those activities. For example, if the person enjoys cooking but struggles with following a recipe, the caregiver can simplify the recipe or pre-measure ingredients.

Despite the challenges of dementia caregiving, there are many opportunities for caregivers to find joy and meaning in the journey. By focusing on the present moment, creating opportunities for engagement and connection, prioritizing self-care, celebrating the person with dementia, and seeking out support and resources, caregivers can find fulfillment and purpose in their role as a caregiver.

It's also important to remember that finding joy in the journey is not a one-size-fits-all solution. What brings joy to one caregiver may not be the same for another. Caregivers should experiment with different strategies and find what works best for them and their loved one. It's also important to acknowledge that finding joy in the journey does not mean ignoring the challenges and difficulties of dementia caregiving.

Caregiving can be emotionally taxing and can require a great deal of patience and resilience. Caregivers should seek out emotional support when needed and not feel guilty about experiencing negative emotions such as sadness, frustration, or anger. One way to address these negative emotions is through mindfulness practices such as meditation, deep breathing, or yoga. These practices can help caregivers cultivate a sense of calm and resilience in the face of difficult emotions and situations.

In addition to mindfulness practices, caregivers can also benefit from cognitive-behavioral therapy (CBT) or other forms of therapy. These therapies can help caregivers identify and change negative thought patterns and develop coping strategies for managing stress and difficult emotions.

Ultimately, finding joy in the journey of dementia caregiving requires a combination of strategies, including focusing on the present moment, creating opportunities for engagement and connection, prioritizing self-care, celebrating the person with dementia, seeking out support and resources, and addressing negative emotions through mindfulness or therapy. By incorporating these strategies into their caregiving routine, caregivers can find purpose and fulfillment in their role and create meaningful moments with their loved one.

THE VASE
by Elizabeth Heller

Thank you, Sarah, for the pottery vase
A thoughtful, beautiful gift!
What better than a tulip
Or a daisy for a lift!
Nature fills our hearts and souls
A simple buttercup
A squirrel or tiny devilish mole
To keep our spirits up
But nothing beats your smile and love
And music fills the air
The sounds surround the atmosphere
And heals with heartful care
I'm blessed to have a daughter
And blessed to have a son
And grandchildren added to the list
of love for everyone!
We have the gift of partners
Who adds to this long list
And loving little creatures
Always to be kissed
(and never to be missed)

And helpers who come daily
With movements quick and swift
Thankfulness forever
It's precious love that's such a gift
Graciousness and heartfulness
And love is in the air
May we be thankful every day
Give love and be aware!

FATUMA KEITA

September 12, 2022

FATUMA

CHAPTER 11

ACCEPTANCE

As we navigate life with a loved one with dementia, one of the biggest challenges we face is coming to terms with the changes that are happening to them and to us. Acceptance is an essential component of finding peace and contentment in this situation. In this chapter, we will explore what acceptance means, why it is important, and how we can cultivate it in our lives.

Acceptance means acknowledging and embracing the reality of our situation, including its challenges and limitations, without resistance or judgment. It is not about resignation or giving up, but rather about finding peace and contentment with what is. Acceptance involves recognizing the things that we cannot control and focusing our energy and attention on the things that we can.

Acceptance is important for several reasons. First, it allows us to let go of our attachment to how things used to be and embrace the present moment as it is. This can help us to reduce stress and anxiety and find a greater sense of calm and peace. Second, acceptance allows us to focus our energy and attention on the things that we can control. When we resist what is happening in our lives, we waste valuable time and energy fighting against something that we cannot change. Acceptance frees us up to focus on the things that we can do to make the situation better. Third, acceptance can help us to build stronger relationships with our loved ones. When we accept them as they are, without judgment or criticism, we create a safe and loving space in which they can feel heard, seen, and valued. This can deepen our connection and bring us closer together.

Cultivating acceptance is an ongoing process that requires patience, compassion, and self-awareness. Here are some strategies that can help us to cultivate acceptance in our lives:

1. Practice Mindfulness: Mindfulness is the practice of paying attention to the present

moment with curiosity and openness, without judgment or distraction. When we practice mindfulness, we learn to observe our experience without trying to change it, which can help us to cultivate a greater sense of acceptance and peace.

2. Connect with Others: Connecting with others who are going through a similar experience can be a powerful way to cultivate acceptance. Support groups, online forums, and social networks can provide us with a safe and supportive space in which we can share our experiences, learn from others, and feel heard and understood.

3. Embrace Self-Compassion: Self-compassion is the practice of treating ourselves with kindness, understanding, and care. When we cultivate self-compassion, we learn to accept ourselves as we are, flaws and all. This can help us to cultivate acceptance in our lives by allowing us to recognize and embrace our own limitations, rather than judging ourselves harshly for them.

4. Let Go of Expectations: Expectations can be a significant barrier to acceptance. When we hold onto expectations of how things should be, we set ourselves up for disappointment and frustration. Instead, we can practice letting go of our expectations and embracing the present moment as it is. This can help us to find greater peace and contentment in our lives.

5. Find Meaning and Purpose: Finding meaning and purpose in our lives can help us to cultivate acceptance by giving us a sense of direction and focus. When we have a clear sense of our values and priorities, we can more easily let go of the things that are outside of our control and focus our energy on the things that matter most to us.

Acceptance is particularly important for caregivers navigating life with a loved one with dementia. It can be challenging to accept the changes that are happening to our loved one, as well as the changes that are happening in our own lives. Here are some ways that cultivating acceptance can benefit caregivers:

1. Reducing Stress and Burnout: Caregiving can be demanding, and it is important to find ways to reduce stress and prevent burnout. Cultivating acceptance can help caregivers to find greater peace and contentment in their role, reducing stress and preventing burnout.

2. Improving Relationships: When caregivers are able to accept their loved one with dementia as they are, without judgment or criticism, it can deepen their connection and improve their relationship. This can lead to greater mutual understanding and empathy, creating a more loving and supportive environment for both the caregiver and the person with dementia.

3. Making Informed Decisions: Acceptance can also help caregivers to make more informed decisions about their loved one's care. When we accept the reality of our situation, including our loved one's limitations and challenges, we can make decisions that are grounded in reality and more likely to be effective.

4. Finding Meaning and Purpose: Cultivating acceptance can help caregivers to find meaning and purpose in their role, by focusing on the things that matter most to them and by recognizing the value of their caregiving role.

In conclusion, acceptance is an essential component of navigating life with a loved one with dementia. It allows us to find peace and contentment in the present moment, to focus our energy on the things that we can control, and to deepen our relationships with our loved ones. Cultivating acceptance is an ongoing process that requires patience, compassion, and self-awareness, but it is a worthwhile endeavor that can bring us greater peace, contentment, and fulfillment in our lives.

THE KIZMAT HOUSE

by Elizabeth Heller

Sarah played a gig last night
A very competent crew
Sarah at the piano with a saxophone
And bass and drummer too
The Kizmat house was easily packed,
The audience was alert and stilled
The magic bounced from corner to bench
The notes complete—fulfilled
Such a joyful evening
With music in the air
How heavenly sounds filled hearts and minds
With everlasting fare
Music is love — music is healing
Music is genuinely rare
May music fill the earth and sky
And feed souls everywhere!

CHAPTER 12

LETTING GO

As my mother's disease progressed, I had to come to terms with the fact that she was not going to get better and let go of the hope that she would recover and return to her former self. This was a difficult realization, but it also allowed me to focus on what was important—spending quality time with my mother and making the most of our remaining time together.

As dementia progresses, caregivers may face difficult decisions about letting go and transitioning their loved one to a care facility or eventually, hospice. In this chapter, we will explore the challenges of letting go and provide strategies for caregivers to navigate this difficult process. The decision to let go can be emotionally challenging for caregivers, as it may feel like a failure or a betrayal of their loved one. Caregivers may feel guilty or anxious about leaving their loved one in the care of others. However, it's important to remember that letting go is not a failure, but rather a necessary step in providing the best possible care for the person with dementia.

It's completely understandable to feel guilty when considering finding another place for your loved one to live, especially if you've been caring for them in your own home. It's important to remember that guilt is a natural emotion that arises from a sense of responsibility and care for our loved ones. Sometimes, the best decision for your loved one's care and well-being may not be the easiest one to make.

Caring for someone with memory loss can be incredibly challenging, both physically and emotionally. It's not uncommon for caregivers to experience burnout, exhaustion, and stress, which can take a toll on their own health and well-being. It's essential to recognize when you've reached your limits and need to consider alternative care options for your mother.

It's important to remember that finding another place for your mother to live doesn't mean you're abandoning her or not fulfilling your duty as a caregiver. It simply means that you're acknowledging your limitations and making the best decision for your mother's care.

One way to ease the emotional burden of letting go is to focus on finding the right care facility or hospice. Caregivers should research and visit different facilities, ask questions, and talk to staff and other families to get a sense of the care provided. By finding a facility or hospice that aligns with their values and goals for care, caregivers can feel more comfortable and confident in their decision to let go.

Another way is to involve the person with dementia in the decision-making process as much as possible. Depending on their level of cognitive function, they may have a say in where they want to live and what type of care they prefer. It's important to respect the wishes of and empower the person with memory loss as much as possible. When discussing the future and plans for long-term care, one must also take into account the individual's wishes and preferences as much as possible. This may involve the pros and cons of different options with the person, explaining why a move may be necessary, and offering reassurance that they will still be loved and cared for. By involving the person with dementia in the decision-making process, caregivers can help them feel empowered and respected, which can reduce feelings of guilt and anxiety. By involving the individual with dementia in the planning process, caregivers can help to alleviate some of the fear and anxiety that may be driving their denial.

Whenever I would bring up the topic of finding another place for her to live, my mother would get upset and say things like, "Don't throw me away!" In this case, it's important to approach the situation with empathy and understanding. It's understandable that she may feel hurt or abandoned, but it's important to communicate to her that your decision is based on what's best for her care and well-being.

Here are some tips on how to approach the conversation with your loved one:

1. Acknowledge their feelings: Let your loved one know that you understand how they feel and that their feelings are valid. You can

say something like, "I understand that this is a difficult decision for you, and I know that it may feel like we're throwing you away. But please know that we're doing this because we want what's best for your care and well-being."

2. Explain your reasoning: Be clear and honest about your reasons for considering alternative care options. Explain that caring for them has been challenging and that you want to ensure that she receives the best possible care.

3. Involve them in the decision-making process: Depending on their level of cognitive function, involve your loved one in the decision-making process as much as possible. Ask her about their preferences and try to find a care facility that meets their specific needs and desires.

4. Offer reassurance: Let them know that you will still be there for them and that you will continue to visit and spend time with them. Offer reassurance that you love them and

that your decision is not a reflection of your feelings toward her.

5. Seek professional help: If your loved one is having a difficult time accepting the decision, consider seeking professional help. A therapist or counselor can help them work through their feelings and come to terms with the decision.

The decision to find another place for your loved one to live is not an easy one, but it's important to prioritize their care and well-being. With empathy, understanding, and clear communication, you can help your loved one understand that your decision is based on your love and concern.

Caregivers may also benefit from seeking out emotional support during the process of letting go. This may include attending support groups, talking to a therapist, or reaching out to friends and family for support. It could also mean prioritizing self-care activities such as exercise, meditation, or spending time with friends and family. Caregivers should take breaks when needed and seek out respite care to prevent burnout and emotional exhaustion. By processing their emotions and receiving support, caregivers can navigate the difficult process of letting go with more resilience and strength.

Finally, it's important for caregivers to remember that letting go does not mean abandoning their loved one. Caregivers can continue to provide emotional support and visit regularly, which can help maintain the bond with their loved one. By recognizing the importance of their continued presence and involvement, caregivers can let go with the knowledge that they are still a vital part of their loved one's life.

In summary, letting go can be a difficult and emotional process for caregivers of loved ones with dementia. However, by focusing on finding the right care facility or hospice, involving the person with dementia in the decision-making process, seeking out emotional support, taking care of themselves, and recognizing the importance of their continued involvement, caregivers can navigate the process with greater resilience and strength.

GIVING THANKS AGAIN

by Elizabeth Heller

The sun is out—the cats are free
How lucky can we be?
Family and friends—kind with love
Food is plentiful thank the stars above
Grandkids, son and daughter too
We all have so much me and you!
Helpers kind—health is good
We try to do what's what we should
We walk, we talk we're blessed indeed
We've plenty—we have all we need
We breathe fresh air, we're free to be
Free to be You and Me!
We must give thanks to the U.S.A.
A country free—free every day
Thanks are due to all our friends
Our loved ones too—we make amends
We love, we share, we laugh, and be
We grow our crops, we thank each tree
Thank Fatouma, Marie and Flor
And thank our kitties, Rafa and Thor!
Asher Levi—our doggie too—
And all who care for me and you!

CHAPTER 13

THE POWER OF LOVE

In this chapter, we will explore the role of love in caregiving and how it can help both the caregiver and the person with dementia navigate the challenges of this journey. Through it all, the one thing that sustained me was the power of love. My love for my mother and her love for me gave me the strength to keep going, even in the darkest of times. Caring for someone with dementia is not easy, but it is also a profound and meaningful experience. It is a chance to show love and compassion in its purest form. It is a chance to make a difference in someone's life and to leave a lasting legacy of love.

For a person with memory loss, love can provide a sense of security and comfort. Even as their memory and cognitive abilities decline, your loved one can still feel the love and care of their caregiver, which reduces feelings of anxiety, fear, and confusion. Love can also provide a sense of continuity and identity, as the person with dementia may still recognize their caregiver and feel a sense of connection to their past.

The difficulty of caregiving can place a strain on the caregiver's ability to express love and affection. Caregivers may feel unappreciated or unrecognized for their efforts due to their loved one becoming less able to communicate their needs or reciprocate affection.

One way for caregivers to express love and affection is through nonverbal communication. This can include physical touch, such as holding hands, hugging, or massaging, which can help to promote a sense of calm and connection.

Another way for caregivers to express love is through reminiscing and sharing memories. Caregivers can share stories and photos of shared experiences, which can help to reinforce the person with dementia's sense of identity and provide a sense of comfort and connection. Reminiscing can also help caregivers to feel more connected to their loved one and provide a sense of purpose and meaning.

Love can also provide a sense of resilience and strength during difficult moments. Caregiving can be emotionally and physically exhausting, and the stress and strain can sometimes lead to feelings of burnout or resentment. However, by focusing on the power of love, caregivers can find strength and resilience to persevere through difficult moments. This may involve reminding themselves of the love and connection they share with their loved one, or seeking out support and encouragement from others who understand the challenges of caregiving. It's of utmost importance for caregivers to practice self-love and self-care. Caregiving can be all-consuming, and caregivers may neglect their own needs in order to provide care for their loved one. However, by practicing self-care and self-love, caregivers can recharge their emotional and physical reserves, which can help them to provide better care for their loved one. This may involve prioritizing self-care activities such as exercise, meditation, or spending time with friends and family. Caregivers should also take breaks when needed and seek out respite care to prevent burnout and emotional exhaustion.

It's also important to acknowledge that the experience of love in caregiving can be complex and multifaceted. While love can provide comfort and connection, it can also be a source of conflict and tension. For example, caregivers may struggle with feelings of resentment or frustration towards their loved one, or may feel guilty about not being able to provide the level of care they would like. It's important for caregivers to acknowledge and address these complex emotions, rather than denying or suppressing them. This may involve seeking out support from a therapist or support group or simply allowing themselves to feel and process their emotions in a healthy and constructive way. I mention this in almost every chapter because it is so important to get support for yourself as self-help should be prioritized.

In addition, caregivers should also be mindful of the impact of dementia on their loved one's ability to express love and affection. As dementia progresses, the person with dementia may become less able to recognize or express their emotions, which can be difficult for caregivers to navigate. It's important for caregivers to be patient and understanding, and to focus on finding new ways to connect and communicate with their loved one. This may involve adjusting their expectations and being open to new ways of expressing love and affection, such as through music, art, or sensory activities. Ultimately, the power of love in caregiving lies in its ability to provide a sense of connection, purpose, and meaning in the midst of a challenging and often unpredictable journey. By focusing on love and connection, caregivers can navigate the challenges of dementia with grace and compassion, while also finding strength and resilience to care for themselves and their loved ones.

In summary, love is a powerful force that can provide comfort and strength to both the person with dementia and their caregiver. By focusing on non-verbal communication, reminiscing, and self-care, caregivers can express their love and maintain their emotional connection with their loved one, even as dementia progresses. By recognizing the power of love, caregivers can find resilience and strength to navigate the challenges of caregiving with grace and compassion.

OUR CHRISTMAS TREE

by Elizabeth Heller

Our Christmas tree is a glittery sight
Our hearts are filled with colors bright
The room exudes both care and love
As stars keep twinkling high above
Sarah plays such magnificent tunes
And music sends chills and startles the moons
Erik is busy preparing Xmas fires
To glowing expressions for Christmas choirs
Lara, Lorenzo, and Sarah of course
Keep Asher prancing with nary remorse
Songs are sprinkling holiday dreams
Love opens our home to heartfelt scenes
Piano delights bounces and startles the soul
Sending love, kisses, and joy—our holiday goal!
Rafa and Thor share kittenly joy
For each Christmas girl and holiday boy
All the adults are tickled pink
As though each soul is giddy with drink
Enjoy the moment, it's rare and it's hot
We give what we wish and get what we've got!

CONCLUSION

Caring for a loved one with dementia is a journey that is both challenging and rewarding. It is a chance to show love and compassion in its purest form and to make a difference in someone's life. In this book, I have shared my personal journey with my mother through the maze of memory loss. I have shared the challenges, emotions, and experiences that come with caring for a loved one with dementia, as well as the practical tips and strategies that I have found helpful in managing the daily challenges of caring for someone with dementia.

My hope is that this book will provide comfort, support, and inspiration to those who are caring for someone with dementia. I hope that it will remind them that they are not alone and that their love and compassion are making a difference in someone's life. Caregiving for a loved one with dementia is a difficult and often thankless task. It requires immense patience, compassion, and dedication, and can often feel overwhelming and isolating. But it's also a journey that is filled with moments of beauty, connection, and love. By approaching caregiving with an open heart and a willingness to learn and grow, caregivers can find meaning and purpose in their role, even in the most challenging moments.

Throughout this book, we have emphasized the importance of self-care as a critical component of effective caregiving. Caregivers must prioritize their own physical, emotional, and mental health in order to be able to provide the best possible care for their loved one. This may involve taking breaks, seeking out support from friends, family, or professionals, or simply making time for activities and hobbies that bring joy and relaxation. We have emphasized the importance of finding joy in the journey, even amidst the challenges and hardships of caregiving. Caregivers must be open to new experiences and opportunities, and be willing to find meaning and beauty in unexpected places. This may involve engaging in creative activities with their loved one, seeking out support from others, or simply focusing on the present moment and finding joy in the small things.

In addition, we have explored the many challenges that caregivers face when communicating with a loved one with dementia. It's important for caregivers to be patient, empathetic, and creative in finding new ways to connect and communicate with their loved one. This may involve using non-verbal cues, such as touch or facial expressions, or engaging in activities that are meaningful and enjoyable for both caregiver and loved one.

We have also highlighted the emotional toll of caregiving, which can be significant and often overwhelming. Caregivers must be mindful of their own emotions and seek out support and resources when needed. This may involve talking to a therapist, joining a support group, or simply reaching out to friends and family for help.

Additionally, we have explored the power of love in caregiving, which is perhaps the most important and transformative force of all. Love has the power to provide comfort, connection, and meaning in even the most difficult and trying moments of caregiving. By focusing on love and connection, caregivers can navigate the challenges of dementia with grace and compassion, while also finding strength and resilience to care for themselves and their loved ones.

As we come to the end of this book, it's important to reflect on the many challenges and rewards of caregiving for a loved one with dementia. We have explored the diagnosis process, the adjustments required to cope with the new normal, the challenges of communication, the emotional toll of caregiving, the importance of finding joy in the journey, the process of letting go, and the power of love. Through it all, we have emphasized the importance of self-care, seeking support, and cultivating resilience in the face of adversity.

As we move forward, it's important to recognize that the needs of caregivers and their loved ones will continue to evolve and change over time. New challenges will arise, and new solutions and strategies will need to be developed. It's important for caregivers to remain open to new ideas, resources, and support as they navigate this journey. We encourage all caregivers to prioritize their own well-being, seek out support and resources, and approach caregiving with compassion, patience, and an open heart. Caregiving for a loved one with dementia is not easy, but it can also be a journey of growth, transformation, and love. We wish all caregivers the strength and resilience to navigate this journey with grace and compassion, and we thank them for their dedication and love.

Finally, I would like to express my deepest gratitude to all the caregivers who have shared their stories, experiences, and insights with me. Your willingness to open your hearts and share your journeys has been both humbling and inspiring. I hope that this book serves as a tribute to your love and dedication and that it helps to raise awareness and understanding about the challenges you face.

I would also like to thank the healthcare professionals, researchers, and advocates who are working tirelessly to improve the lives of those affected by dementia. Your commitment and dedication to this cause are truly inspiring, and we are honored to be a part of this community. I hope that this book serves as a source of comfort, support, and inspiration for all those affected by dementia. May it serve as a reminder of the power of love, the resilience of the human spirit, and the importance of compassion and empathy in all aspects of life.

I hope that this book has offered practical strategies and tools for caregivers, as well as emotional support and validation for the challenges they may face. I also hope that this book has helped to raise awareness about dementia and its impact on families and caregivers.

In conclusion, caregiving for a loved one with dementia is a complex and challenging journey, but it is also a journey that is filled with moments of beauty, connection, and love. By approaching caregiving with an open heart and a willingness to learn and grow, caregivers can find meaning and purpose in their role, even in the most difficult moments. It is my hope that this book has provided guidance, support, and inspiration to all those who are caring for a loved one with memory loss.

RESOURCES

Here is a list of resources that may be helpful for people who need support in caring for a loved one with memory loss. These resources can provide valuable information and support for caregivers of people with dementia. It's important for caregivers to take care of themselves and seek help when needed, and these resources can help make that process easier.

1. Alzheimer's Association: This is a nonprofit organization that provides education, support, and resources for people with Alzheimer's disease and their caregivers. Their website offers information on the disease, caregiving, and support services. There is also a 24/7 hotline: (800) 272-3900

2. National Institute on Aging: This organization provides information on aging and health, including dementia and caregiving. Their website offers resources for caregivers, such as tips for managing daily tasks and finding support.

3. Family Caregiver Alliance: This organization offers resources and support for caregivers of people with dementia, including information on caregiving, legal and financial issues, and finding local support groups.

4. AgingCare.com: This website offers resources and support for caregivers of older adults, including those with dementia. Their forums allow caregivers to connect and share advice and experiences.

5. Caregiver Action Network: This organization provides support and resources for family caregivers, including those caring for someone with dementia. Their website offers information on caregiving, advocacy, and support services.

6. AARP: This organization offers information and resources for caregivers of older adults, including those with dementia. Their website offers tips and advice on caregiving, legal and financial issues, and finding support.

7. Dementia Care Central: This website offers information and resources for caregivers of people with dementia, including tips for managing behaviors, finding support, and coping with the emotional challenges of caregiving.

8. National Alliance for Caregiving: This organization provides support and resources for family caregivers, including those caring for someone with dementia. Their website offers information on caregiving, advocacy, and support services.

9. Eldercare Locator: This service connects caregivers with local resources and services, including support groups, respite care, and other community-based programs.

10. Local senior centers: Many senior centers offer support groups and educational programs for caregivers of older adults, including those with dementia.

ADDENDUM

We have so very much for which to be grateful! So many glorious years of joyous, loving, adventurous times together—first— and then as a family—loving, happy, hopeful, and appreciative! Our goal is to be caring family members, to listen to one another, and to be grateful! And thankful! For our lives both as family members and as individuals. May we continue to be heartful, close, and loving.

With love and gratefulness,
Elizabeth